A CINEMATIC HISTORY of SCI-FI & FANTASY

Published by Raintree, a division of Reed Elsevier, Inc.
Chicago, Illinois

Customer Service 888-363-4266
Visit our website at www.raintreelibrary.com

A CINEMATIC HISTORY OF SCI-FI & FANTASY
was produced by

David West 🕱 Children's Books
7 Princeton Court
55 Felsham Road
London SW15 1AZ

Designer: David West
Editor: Rowan Lawton, Kate Newport
Picture Research: Gail Bushnell

09 08 07 06 05
10 9 8 7 6 5 4 3 2 1

Library of Congress Cataloging-in-Publication Data
Wilshin, Mark
    A cinematic history of sci-fi & fantasy / Mark Wilshin.
        p. cm.
    Includes bibliographical references and index.
    ISBN 1-4109-2011-9 (lib. bdg.-hard. : alk. paper)
    1.Science fiction films--History and criticism. 2. Fantasy films--
History and criticism. I. Title: Cinematic history of sci-fi and
fantasy. II.Title.
    PN1995.9.S26W56 2005
    791.43'615--dc22
                                        2005009511

Printed and bound in China

Acknowledgements
The author and publishers are grateful to the
following for permission to reproduce copyright
material:
cover m, 20TH CENTURY FOX / THE KOBAL COLLECTION /
DIGITAL DOMAIN; cover r UFA / THE KOBAL COLLECTION; cover t
WARNER BROS / THE KOBAL COLLECTION; 3, LUCASFILM/20TH
CENTURY FOX / THE KOBAL COLLECTION; 4l, Photo By EVERETT
COLLECTION / REX FEATURES; 4r, NEW LINE CINEMA / THE
KOBAL COLLECTION; 5r CHRIS LEE PROD/SQUARE CO / THE
KOBAL COLLECTION;6tr, Photo By EVERETT COLLECTION / REX
FEATURES; 6b, MELIES / THE KOBAL COLLECTION;7t, Photo By REX
FEATURES; 7bl, Photo By EVERETT COLLECTION / REX FEATURES;
7br, RKO / THE KOBAL COLLECTION; 8tr, Photo By SNAP / REX
FEATURES; 8bl, UNIVERSAL / THE KOBAL COLLECTION; 8br, Photo
By SNAP / REX FEATURES; 9t, Photo By EVERETT COLLECTION /
REX FEATURES; 9b, 20TH CENTURY FOX / THE KOBAL
COLLECTION; 10t, Photo By SNAP / REX FEATURES; 10b, Photo By
C.20THC.FOX/ EVERETT / REX FEATURES;11-12t, Photo By
C.20THC.FOX/EVERETT / REX FEATURES; 11r, Photo By REX
FEATURES; 11b, Photo By SIPA PRESS / REX FEATURES;12t, Photo By
SNAP / REX FEATURES; 12bl, Photo By C. WARNER BR / EVERETT /
REX FEATURES; 12br, 20TH CENTURY FOX / THE KOBAL
COLLECTION / DIGITAL DOMAIN; 13t, Photo By REX FEATURES;
13bl, Photo By EVERETT COLLECTION / REX FEATURES; 13br, Photo
By C.WARNER BR/EVERETT / REX FEATURES; 14tr, GEORGE PAL
PRODS / THE KOBAL COLLECTION; 14m, Photo By EVERETT
COLLECTION / REX FEATURES; 14b, Photo By EVERETT
COLLECTION / REX FEATURES; 15t, Photo By C.20THC.FOX/
EVERETT / REX FEATURES; 15m, MGM / THE KOBAL COLLECTION;
15b, Photo By EVERETT COLLECTION / REX FEATURES;16-17m,
LUCASFILM/20TH CENTURY FOX / THE KOBAL COLLECTION; 16bl,
(c) LUCASFILM LTD. & TM. All rights reserved. Used with permission;
16br, LUCASFILM/20TH CENTURY FOX / THE KOBAL COLLECTION;
17t, Photo By C.LUCASFILM/EVERETT / REX FEATURES; 17bl,
LUCASFILM / THE KOBAL COLLECTION; 17br, THE KOBAL
COLLECTION / LUCASFILM/20TH CENTURY FOX; 18t, Photo By
SNAP / REX FEATURES; 18b, UFA / THE KOBAL COLLECTION; 19tr,
MGM / THE KOBAL COLLECTION; 19tl, 20TH CENTURY
FOX/DREAMWORKS / THE KOBAL COLLECTION; 19b, WARNER
BROS / THE KOBAL COLLECTION; 20t, Photo By SNAP / REX
FEATURES; 20b, AMBLIN/UNIVERSAL / THE KOBAL COLLECTION;
21t, WARNER BROS / THE KOBAL COLLECTION; 21b, COLUMBIA
TRISTAR / THE KOBAL COLLECTION / CENTROPOLIS EFFECTS; 22t,
Photo By EVERETT COLLECTION / REX FEATURES; 22b, THE KOBAL
COLLECTION / FILMS ANDRE PAULVE; 23t, 20TH CENTURY FOX /
THE KOBAL COLLECTION; 23bl, Photo By LIPNITSKI/ROGER-
VIOLLET / REX FEATURES; 23br, WARNER BROS / THE KOBAL
COLLECTION / MOUNTAIN, PETER; 24t, COLUMBIA / THE KOBAL
COLLECTION; 24bl, Photo By EVERETT COLLECTION / REX
FEATURES; 24br, Photo By REX FEATURES; 25t, UMBRELLA / THE
KOBAL COLLECTION; 25b, GABRIELLA MEROS / REX FEATURES;
26t, Photo By SNAP / REX FEATURES; 26b, WARNER BROS/DC
COMICS / THE KOBAL COLLECTION; 27t, Photo By REX FEATURES;
27l, WARNER BROS/DC COMICS / THE KOBAL COLLECTION; 27br,
Photo By C.COLUMBIA/EVERETT / REX FEATURES; 28t, Photo By
C.20THC.FOX/EVERETT / REX FEATURES; 28b, Photo By REX
FEATURES; 29t, Photo By EVERETT COLLECTION / REX FEATURES;
29r, TOUHOKU SHINSHA / THE KOBAL COLLECTION; 30t,
COLUMBIA / THE KOBAL COLLECTION, 30m, Photo By
C.TRISTAR/EVERETT / REX FEATURES.

Every effort has been made to contact copyright holders of any material
reproduced in this book. Any omissions will be rectified in subsequent
printings if notice is given to the publisher.

*An explanation of difficult words can be
found in the glossary on page 31.*

A CINEMATIC HISTORY of SCI-FI & FANTASY

MARK WILSHIN

Raintree
Chicago, Illinois

CONTENTS

INTRODUCTION

*Tales of warring planets, aliens, and robots have existed since the novels of Jules Verne and H.G. Wells in the 19th century, yet it is the science fiction movie that has created lasting images of flying saucers and future worlds. From early cinematic dreams of flying to the moon to nightmares of modern technology, science fiction has recorded the hopes and fears of the human race from age to age. Most popular at times of national and international crisis, science fiction exposed America's fear of **communism** during the **Cold War**, as well as recording each new generation's fear of technology. Yet in order to recreate these imaginary spaceships, **cyborgs**, and aliens, science fiction has constantly had to pioneer advances in technology, from early models and miniatures to the computerized special effects of today.*

FANTASIES OF EARLY CINEMA

Optimistic about the new possibilities of modern technology, early science fiction movies created fantastic visions of the future with humans mastering the laws of nature and crossing the final frontier into space.

SCIENCE FICTION IS BORN

Georges Méliès' *A Trip to the Moon* (1902) is the most famous silent science fiction film, but it was not the first. In Wallace McCutcheon's *The X-Ray Mirror* (1899), a young woman admires herself wearing a new hat in a shop mirror. Her reflection changes and she sees herself as a ballet dancer. The film was the first to link science fiction, set design, and special effects.

GEORGES MÉLIÈS

In 1895, when French magician Georges Méliès attended the Lumière Brothers' première of the Cinematograph, a machine that could project films for an audience, he knew what these films were missing—a story. Méliès saw that he could use film-trick photography and painted scenery in his act.

A TRIP TO THE MOON (1902)

With A Trip to the Moon, *Méliès created the first story in film history. Loosely based on the novel by Jules Verne, it is a comic sci-fi film. The astronauts are old men in top hats who fly to the moon in a steel space capsule. Méliès combined the scenes using editing techniques such as stop-motion and lap dissolves, in which the old scene fades as the new one appears.*

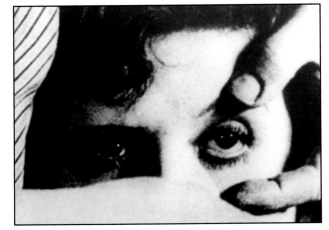

UN CHIEN ANDALOU (1929)

Luis Buñuel collaborated with Salvador Dalí to create a surrealist fantasy. With its seemingly unconnected sequences of a man dragging two grand pianos and a hand with ants coming out of a hole in it, Un Chien Andalou has no direct meaning. Viewers decide upon their own meaning as they watch.

ROCKET SCIENCE

In the 1920s, as air travel was perfected, space travel began to capture the popular imagination and rocket science became the new challenge for pioneering scientists. Unlike Méliès' comic vision of aristocratic astronauts landing in the man in the moon's eye, Fritz Lang's *Frau im Mond* (1928) gave a more realistic portrait of the science of space travel. With the collaboration of German rocket scientists, Lang showed the journey to the moon in a more realistic way. He included the stage rocket, as well as the effects of acceleration and weightlessness. In this film, it was Lang who used the first rocket launch countdown. Years later, real rockets would launch using a similar countdown.

KING KONG (1933)

King Kong, *the fantastic story of people fighting a giant gorilla, was a welcome escape from the reality of the **Great Depression**. Yet it was Willis O'Brien's pioneering special effects that led to the film's tremendous success.*

THE END OF THE WORLD

*During the **Cold War** of the 1950s, the threat of **communism** and nuclear war reached its peak, creating a boom in science fiction. This ranged from paranoid ideas of alien invasion to environmental and nuclear disasters.*

SPACE INVADERS

In 1950s sci-fi films, alien armies were used to represent the threat many people felt from the communist **Soviet Union**, an unknown enemy determined to destroy U.S. values. In *The War of the Worlds* (1953) and *This Island Earth* (1955), aliens intend to take over Earth, unable to be stopped by an **atomic bomb**. This revealed the United States' fear of losing the race between nations to develop weapons.

THE WAR OF THE WORLDS (1953)

The War of the Worlds shows the fall of the world's major cities to a Martian army, while scientists race to develop a weapon to defeat them.

ORSON WELLES

Science fiction has been linked to a real fear of alien invasion since the radio broadcast of The War of the Worlds in 1938. Welles created panic with a series of live news bulletins in which he read H.G. Wells' sci-fi novel, convincing ordinary Americans that Martians really were invading.

THE DAY THE EARTH CAUGHT FIRE (1961)

In this film the U.S.A. and the U.S.S.R. launch nuclear bombs at the North and South poles, making Earth fall off its axis and race toward the Sun.

DR. STRANGELOVE OR: HOW I LEARNED TO STOP WORRYING AND LOVE THE BOMB (1963)

Stanley Kubrick's dark comedy of nuclear war tells the story of a mad general launching nuclear missiles at the Soviet Union. Three men, the U.S. President, a British captain, and a Nazi nuclear expert Dr. Strangelove, all played by Peter Sellers, try to divert the bombs and save the world. The film makes fun of military and political powers that have created missiles that can destroy Earth.

THE END IS NEAR!

With the atomic bomb and nuclear war as a constant threat to society after World War II (1939–1945), there were many Cold War bomb movies. Films like *Five* (1951) and *On the Beach* (1959) show survivors of a **nuclear holocaust,** commenting on society's need to live peacefully. Other films like *Fail Safe* (1964) show how easily missiles could be launched by electrical malfunction, and how Russians and Americans must work to avert war. *Mad Max* (1979) portrays a world of violence, where only the ruthless survive. Other films like *The Day After Tomorrow* (2004) use global warming as the source of environmental disaster.

THE DAY AFTER TOMORROW (2004)

The Day After Tomorrow *imagines the horror of a new ice age. In it New York is torn apart by tidal waves and tornardoes. This is a vision of a future destroyed by ecological threats.*

ALIENS

Aliens have been depicted in many ways during the history of cinema, from the **humanoid** *appearance of the first on-screen alien in Algol (1920) to the mucus-dripping frights of the Alien series.*

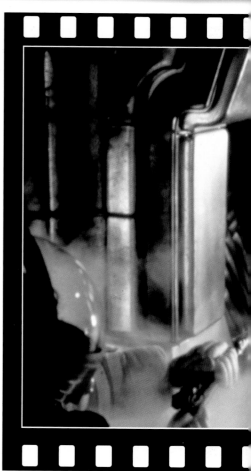

THE DAY THE EARTH STOOD STILL (1951)

An alien and a robot come from space to warn people to stop their nuclear frenzy or Earth will be reduced to burned ashes.

ALIEN AGGRESSORS

The Thing From Another World (1951) is often considered to be the film that launched the craze of **Cold War** sci-fi films about monsters intent on destroying humanity. It tells the story of an alien spaceship discovered in the Arctic. When the pilot thaws out, he goes on a rampage killing everyone in sight.

INDEPENDENCE DAY (1996)

This alien invasion echoes the invasion movies of the Cold War, updating them with CGI sequences showing the realistic destruction of U.S. landmarks.

Alien (1979)

In Ridley Scott's famous Alien, *a commercial mining spaceship receives what they believe is an S.O.S message from a distant planet. Upon landing they find a derelict ship, now the breeding ground for thousands of alien eggs. The* Alien *series questions the ethics of colonization and business, while the aliens are depicted as a threat to human biology itself, when a man gives birth to an alien monster.*

E.T. (1982)

Created by sculptor Carlo Rimbaldi, E.T. is a friendly, 600–800 year old alien, who was accidentally left behind on Earth. A young boy befriends him and helps E.T. get back to his spaceship before he is captured by the police.

INTERSTELLAR VISITORS

Modern films like *Independence Day* (1996) continued the trend of alien invaders wanting to take over Earth. However, not all aliens were evil monsters. In *The Day the Earth Stood Still* (1951), the alien Klaatu and his robot Gort are the film's real heroes, delivering a wise warning against nuclear war. As interest in the extraterrestrial grew and U.F.O. (unidentified flying object) sightings increased, so did Hollywood's attitude toward aliens, resulting in the supernatural encounters of *Close Encounters of the Third Kind* (1977) and *E.T.* (1982). In *Close Encounters of the Third Kind*, Ray Neary experiences visions after an encounter with a U.F.O.

MARS ATTACKS! (1997)

A tribute to 1950s sci-fi movies, Mars Attacks! *shows Earth invaded by Martians who have come to destroy it just for fun. Tim Burton* satirizes *American society as his aliens ray gun everyone from the president to the ordinary citizen.*

FORBIDDEN PLANET (1956)

The dressmaking robot named Robby represents an optimistic belief in a domestic, mechanical servant.

ROBOTS

Robots reveal the desire to create life. As technology develops, so does the vision of the robot, from the 1950s box of mechanics to androids, organic machines with feelings and a human appearance.

THE ROBOT REVOLUTION

Making their first film appearance in *The Master Mystery* (1919), evil on-screen robots later became friendlier in films such as *Forbidden Planet* (1956). As society's faith in modern technology faded, film robots began to rebel. In *Westworld* (1973) and *I, Robot* (2004), robots revolt against humans, exposing society's anxieties about living in a computerized world.

BLADE RUNNER (1982)

*Ridley Scott's blend of sci-fi and **film noir** presents a dark and grimy Los Angeles in the year 2019, home to androids and humans. Adapted from Philip K. Dick's novel <u>Do Androids Dream of Electric Sheep?</u> the film shows the android's desire to be human. As policeman Deckard struggles to maintain his humanity, the film questions what it means to be human.*

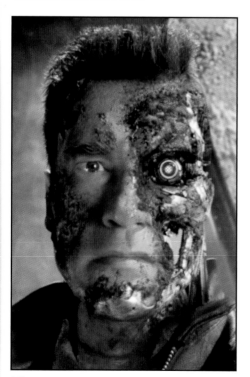

THE TERMINATOR (1984)

*Man's fear of the machine—the Terminator is a ruthless **cyborg** sent from the future to kill the mother of a future revolutionary.*

ANDROIDS AND CLONES

Humanoid robots, like the dutiful housewives of *The Stepford Wives* (1975 and 2004), question discrimination, such as sexism. Films of **clones** and androids, like *Gattaca* (1997) and *Code 46* (2004), where human life is artificially created, make us ask what it means to be human, exploring feelings, dreams, and love.

I, Robot (2004)

AI (2001)

In the dark future of Artificial Intelligence: AI, *the artificial (or 'mecha') boy, David, wants desperately to become a real boy and be loved by his adopted mother.*

SPACE & TIME

*The United States and the **Soviet Union** were in fierce competition to be the first country to land a man on the moon. For those caught up in national **patriotism**, films about moon landings and rocket launches were popular crowd-pleasers.*

THE SPACE RACE

In *Destination Moon* (1950) and *Conquest of Space* (1955), space is the final frontier to be conquered, full of drama and exciting machinery. However, when the astronaut Neil Armstrong made the first moon landing in 1969, films such as *Capricorn One* (1978) and *The Right Stuff* (1983) began to look at some worrying aspects of the space program, including some people's theories that the moon landing was a hoax.

DESTINATION MOON (1950)

In Destination Moon, *a space mission is financed by U.S. companies, determined to beat the Russians. The film realistically predicted the launch, spacesuits, and the moon landing.*

ARTHUR C. CLARKE

*A sci-fi author and inventor, Clarke wrote the short story '*The Sentinel*' that inspired director Stanley Kubrick's film* 2001: A Space Odyssey *(1968). They worked together on the screenplay to create a film of outstanding intelligence and beauty that has left viewers puzzled over its meaning.*

2001: A SPACE ODYSSEY (1968)

Based on Arthur C. Clarke's story, 2001: A Space Odyssey *looks at the evolution of humans. Millions of years ago, peace-loving apes find a mysterious stone that begins their existence as violent hunters. Many years later, another stone is found on the moon. Is this the next evolutionary stage for humans? Stanley Kubrick takes a look at the nature of humans, violent and greedy, yet capable of change.*

SOLARIS (2002)

In Solaris, a mysterious ocean on a strange planet is able to materialize a person's dreams and memories, creating an imaginary world more attractive to them than reality.

In 1995, *Apollo 13* recaptured the drama of space travel, in which a routine flight to the moon became a fight for survival.

TIME TRAVEL

Yet it was not just the science and excitement of landing on the moon that fueled films about space travel. The possibility of traveling to other dimensions in space and time turned the space film into a discussion about humanity, **evolution,** and the limits of memory.

In *The Time Machine* (1960 & 2002), an inventor is determined to prove time travel is possible. He invents a time machine that sends him 800,000 years into the future where he finds humans divided and fighting one another.

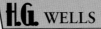

H.G. WELLS

Inspired by author Jules Verne's novels of discovery and exploration, Herbert George Wells wrote many sci-fi novels that have been made into films, including The Invisible Man *(1933),* The Time Machine *(1960 & 2002) and* The War of the Worlds *(1953 & 2005). Wells used his novels to look for ways to improve human society.*

BACK TO THE FUTURE (1985)

When Marty McFly travels back to the 1950s in a mad scientist's converted sports car, he must set his parents on the road to love before he misses his opportunity to return to life in the 1980s.

STAR WARS

*After the height of the **Cold War** and the drama of the moon landings, science fiction went out of fashion, only to be revolutionized in 1977 by Star Wars. As the sci-fi film evolved into the epic blockbuster, the **communist** alien was replaced by Darth Vader.*

GEORGE LUCAS

George Lucas wrote all the Star Wars films, but he only directed Episode IV (1977) from the original trilogy, a series of three films. With the success of Star Wars, he set up Lucas Films, which includes the famous special effects company, Industrial Light & Magic. In 1994, Lucas began writing a new trilogy, set earlier than the original, which he then directed.

STAR WARS (1977)

Droids C-3P0 and R2D2 are mechanical soldiers that land on Tatooine, sent by Princess Leia to tell the Jedi Knight Obi-Wan Kenobi about the Death Star, a space station that can destroy planets. Luke Skywalker, a farmboy, is desperate to escape Tatooine and joins them in their rebellion against the Empire. Obi-Wan teaches him the ways of the force, then Luke enlists smuggler Han Solo and his alien copilot Chewbacca to help him free Princess Leia from the evil Darth Vader. Star Wars is set "a long time ago, in a galaxy far, far away....."

THE EMPIRE STRIKES BACK (1980)

After Obi-Wan's vision and an attack, the rebels separate. While Jedi Yoda trains Luke, Han Solo and Princess Leia are captured by Darth Vader.

RETURN OF THE JEDI (1983)

The evil Empire constructs a new, indestructible Death Star and the rebels attack. Luke has to defeat Darth Vader to become a true Jedi Knight.

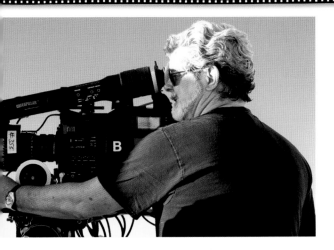

THE EVIL EMPIRE

Unlike some of the 1950s Cold War films, *Star Wars* told its story in human terms, with good finally triumphing over evil. With its fantastic story and incredible special effects, the *Star Wars* trilogy has become an epic. The first film won six Academy Awards®, along with a Special Achievement Award for the sound effects. For example, the sound of the lightsaber weapon is created from a combination of the hum of a movie projector and a tape of an electrical tower.

SPACE OPERA AND CYBERPUNK

Star Wars (1977) is an example of space opera, a term used to describe early sci-fi adventure stories set in space. *Star Wars* focuses on the action and adventure of intergalactic warfare and romance, rather than examining the advances in technology. Technology is shown to be grimy and worn, rather than sleek and sparkling, like in traditional sci-fi. With its dark visions of technology running wild, *Star Wars* anticipated the cyberpunk movement, a type of fast-paced sci-fi typified by bleak, futuristic, and high-tech settings.

THE PHANTOM MENACE (1999)

Part of the second trilogy, set prior to the original films, The Phantom Menace *tells the history of characters from the original* Star Wars *films.*

ATTACK OF THE CLONES (2002)

In Hollywood's first film entirely shot with digital cameras, Anakin leaves the Light Side of the Force with a spectacular battle between good and evil.

BRAVE NEW WORLDS

In film the future is usually a collage of eye scanners, laser guns, and talking computers, but these technological delights are often just the frills of a nightmare world, where humans are isolated and oppressed by machines.

DARK UNDERWORLDS

Since *Metropolis* (1927), films set in the future have reflected contemporary anxieties about technology and the **totalitarian** state. In *Fahrenheit 451* (1966 & 2005), technology is a government tool to control the masses and books are burned for fear of independent thinking. In the bleak totalitarian society of *1984* (1955 & 1984), love is outlawed and society is watched by Big Brother.

METROPOLIS (1927)

Set in the year 2000, Metropolis is a divided city, where the rich live in skyscrapers and travel by plane, while the poor scrape a measly living in the industrial city below ground. After several workers are killed in an accident, Metropolis, the tyrant ruler, plans to stop the rebellion by flooding the city and replacing the workers with robots. Inspired by a visit to New York, Metropolis was the model for all cinematic cities of the future.

SOYLENT GREEN (1973)

Environmental concerns are often projected into the future. Soylent Green (1973) presents the rise in population as well as global warming and pollution, leading to the extinction of natural food.

CINEMA AND THE CITY

Since *Alphaville* (1965), future cities have been created using contemporary architecture made to look strange. *Alphaville* made 1960s Paris into a cold, soulless city. Both *THX 1138* (1971) and *Gattaca* (1997) used the Marin County Civic Center, the ultramodern building of the architect Frank Lloyd Wright, to create a sterile and impersonal future. *Code 46* (2003) shows a divided society, from the modern airports in China to derelict shanty towns in India.

THE MATRIX (1999)

In The Matrix, Neo, *a computer hacker, realizes that his reality is being controlled by a computer and his body is used to power machines. The film shows a world ruled by machines, where human brains are linked to a computer network. The film's pioneering bullet-time effect slowed time so that bullets could be seen as they traveled through the air.*

MONSTERS

Originating from Jules Verne's science fiction novels of exploration and discovery, films of otherworldly monsters and lost worlds depict dramatic adventure pitting the forces of science against the brutal forces of nature.

THEM! (1954)

*After nuclear tests in the desert, giant ants go on a rampage through cities. While the army succeeds in destroying the nest, two flying queen ants escape with some drones. The ants have been seen as representing the threat of **communism** to 1950s America.*

THE CREATURE FEATURE

Prehistoric monster films like *Journey to the Center of the Earth* (1959) and *The Land That Time Forgot* (1975) tell of intrepid adventurers and scientists battling through lost worlds.

GREMLINS (1984)

In Gremlins, *the sci-fi monster is no longer a potent threat to American society and culture, but rather a comic creature content with creating mischief and mayhem.*

NUCLEAR NASTIES

As fear of **nuclear power** peaked in the 1950s, sci-fi films about mutated creatures became popular. These mutated animals had been biologically changed, often into monstrous beings. In *The Beast From 20,000 Fathoms* (1953), a man-eating dinosaur frozen for millions of years thaws out as a result of an Arctic nuclear test. The monster starts making its way down the East Coast, causing mahem. In *It Came From Beneath the Sea* (1955), directed by Robert Gordon, an atomic powered submarine is attacked by a mutant octopus, exposing the dangerous after effects of nuclear radiation.

JURASSIC PARK (1993)

Once scientists discover how to **clone** *dinosaurs from fossilized mosquito blood, a millionaire decides to open a theme park. He invites a select group of scientists to inspect the park. But when someone turns the security system off, the dinosaurs escape their enclosures, and suddenly the visitors must fight to survive. Based on the novel by Michael Crichton,* Jurassic Park *became the most successful film of all time at the box office, earning over $120 million in just ten days.*

GODZILLA (1998)

Adapted from the original Japanese movie Gojira *(1954), the giant, mutant monster Godzilla is created by French* **atomic bomb** *testing in the South Pacific. In a battle between the U.S. military and Godzilla in the streets of Manhattan, Godzilla evokes* King Kong *(1933) and pays tribute to the* **Cold War** *films of the 1950s.*

WIZARDS & WITCHES

Spells and sorcery are not found only in the realm of myth and legend. They can also be found in fantasy films set in the real world, where magic spills into society from fantasy dreamlands.

SOMEWHERE OVER THE RAINBOW

One of the earliest fantasy adventures was *The Wizard of Oz* (1939). It tells the story of Dorothy, who lands in the magical world of Oz with her beloved dog Toto, after her house is carried away by a tornado.

LA BELLE ET LA BÊTE (1946)

When Belle's father gets lost in a forest, he stumbles upon a castle where he picks a rose for Belle. Suddenly the Beast appears demanding the merchant's death unless one of his daughters becomes his prisoner. Belle sacrifices herself and falls in love with the Beast. In La Belle et la Bête (1946), Cocteau creates a magical world where disembodied hands hold candelabras and statues breathe.

In Oz, Dorothy and her dog Toto make friends with the Scarecrow, the Cowardly Lion, and the Tin Man. Together they triumph over the Wicked Witch of the West. *The Wizard of Oz* is divided into two sections, with Kansas shown in black and white, and the fantasyland of Oz shown in bright, intense colors.

MODERN SORCERY

Witches and wizards abound in modern fantasy adventures, too. In *The Witches* (1990) and the *Harry Potter* series, fantasy is combined with the everyday exploits of children as they uncover the evil plots of wizards and witches. In *Harry Potter and the Sorcerer's Stone* (2001), Harry discovers a hidden world of three-headed dogs, elves, and the flying broomstick polo game Quidditch.

EDWARD SCISSORHANDS (1990)

In Tim Burton's Edward Scissorhands (1990), a door-to-door cosmetic salesperson stumbles upon an old mansion inhabited by Edward, a man with scissors for hands. Adopted into her family, Edward adapts to suburban life, cutting hedges and hair. Yet the harmony does not last as society reveals its prejudice and violence towards the strange and the unknown.

JEAN COCTEAU

Cocteau was an artist as well as a writer of poems, plays, novels and films. Focusing on fairy tale and myth, Jean Cocteau created films like La Belle et La Bête *(1946) and* Orphée *(1950). In* Orphée, *the Poet disappears through liquid mirrors into a world where he is part of a risky game with the Princess of Death.*

HARRY POTTER

In Harry Potter and the Sorcerer's Stone *(2001), Harry must prevent Voldemort, a murderous wizard at Hogwarts School of Witchcraft and Wizardry, from stealing the philosopher's stone and gaining eternal life and the restoration of his power.*

Fantasy, Myths, & Legends

Rather than imagining the future of mankind, fantasy films are often rooted in the classical myths of the Greeks and Romans, or Arthurian legends. These trace the adventures of a hero who battles against the forces of evil in a mystical, magical past.

Mythic Quests

Based on a Greek myth, *Jason and the Argonauts* (1963) is the magical adventure of Jason's search for the mythical Golden Fleece that will give him his rightful place on the throne of Thessaly. On his quest, he must defeat harpies, the giant Talos, a seven-headed hydra, and an army of skeletons.

Jason and the Argonauts (1963)
Special effects genius Ray Harryhausen created this fight scene by shooting the live sequence first with the Argonauts fighting thin air. Then, rubber models of the skeletons were added using stop-motion (see page 30).

Excalibur (1981)
Excalibur depicts Arthur's struggle to become king. With the mystical figures of the Lady in the Lake, the wizard Merlin, and the witch Morgana, Excalibur creates a vision of a past age filled with magic and mystery.

The mythical adventures of Sinbad have also been created on film. In *The Seventh Voyage of Sinbad* (1958), Sinbad has to defeat a cyclops, a giant with a single eye in the middle of his forehead, as well as the giant bird Roc, and a dragon, in order to save a princess from an evil wizard.

THE DARK AGES

While the fantastic adventures of Arthurian legend are based on a mythological past, other fantasy films like *Dragonslayer* (1981) and *Legend* (1985) have created their own enchanted medieval kingdoms, in which dragons, unicorns, and demons dwell. In *Legend*, the demonic Lord of Darkness intends to plunge the world into eternal night by killing every unicorn alive.

JABBERWOCKY (1977)

Based on Lewis Carroll's nonsense poem, the film is set in a medieval fantasyland, where Dennis Cooper must slay the Jabberwock to marry the princess. Bloody visuals help to make it a fairy tale of grime and filth.

TERRY GILLIAM

An original member of the comedy team Monty Python's Flying Circus, Terry Gilliam has gone on to make some unique fantasy adventures, including Jabberwocky *(1977),* Time Bandits *(1981), and* Brazil *(1985).*

LORD OF THE RINGS: THE FELLOWSHIP OF THE RING (2001), THE TWO TOWERS (2002), and THE RETURN OF THE KING (2003)

The ring of the Dark Lord, Sauron, has fallen into the hands of Frodo the hobbit, who must cross Middle Earth to Mordor in order to destroy it. Frodo is accompanied by Gandalf the Grey, Legolas the elf, Gimli the dwarf, Aragorn, Boromir, and three hobbits: Samwise, Merry, and Pippin. Peter Jackson's adaptation of Tolkien's novel is a monumental film, examining the nature of humanity and the seductive temptation of power. The trilogy required state of the art special effects, including thousands of digital extras programmed to fight in their own way to create the tremendous battle scenes.

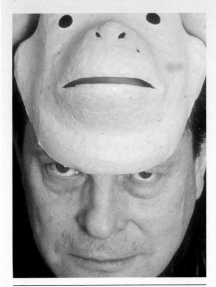

SUPERHEROES

Freak accidents involving deadly waste and radioactive spider bites are some of the ways comic book heroes gain their extraordinary superpowers. But in their fight against the world's most evil villains, these superheroes are on the side of the ordinary people.

THE SUPERHERO'S WORLD

Superhero films are based on the comic books of DC and Marvel comics. Rather than looking to the future, their imagined worlds often recreate a bygone era, such as Gotham City in *Batman* (1989), based on 1930s New York. Planets from outer space feature in other superhero films, such as the planet called Mongo in *Flash Gordon* (1936 & 1980) and the doomed world of Krypton in *Superman* (1978).

FLASH GORDON(1936 & 1980)

Football star Flash Gordon fights arch villain, Ming the Merciless, who aims to destroy Earth, and marry the beautiful Dale Arden.

SUPERMAN (1978)

Before planet Krypton hits its red sun, Jor-El sends his infant son to Earth where his body will become indestructible. The infant crash lands in Smallville, and his adoptive parents teach him about truth and justice. As an adult, he goes to Metropolis, living a double life as a reporter and as Superman, who protects his adopted planet from danger.

X-MEN (2000) and X-MEN 2 (2003)

In a not too distant future, children are born with special powers after their genes are changed by the X-Factor. A group of mutants, the X-Men, make it their mission to heal the hostility between humans and mutants and overcome discrimination.

MAGIC POWERS

Often the most fantastic element of the superhero film is the origin of the hero's superpowers. In *Daredevil* (2003), Matt Murdoch is blinded by poisonous waste, which then improves all his other senses and gives him a secondary radar sight. Both heroes in *Captain America* (1944 and 1991) and *Hulk* (2003) are transformed by scientific experiments. Yet superheroes are not always invincible. Neither Batman nor *The Punisher* (2004) have any superpowers at all.

BATMAN (1989)

Billionaire Bruce Wayne battles the criminals of lawless Gotham city as Batman. Relying on techno-gadgets, he shows the power of an ordinary man.

SPIDERMAN 1 (2001) and SPIDERMAN 2 (2004)

When outcast Peter Parker is bitten by a radioactive spider, his body genetically mutates so he can climb walls and sling webs. During his battles with the Green Goblin and Dr. Octopus (above), Spiderman experiences self doubt.

Animé

Animé films are, in fact, any animated film from Japan. Yet due to their dreamy nature, many fall into the sci-fi and fantasy category. Their imagined worlds range from cyberpunk to fairytale fantasy created by a fusion of hand drawn animation and CGI techniques (see page 30).

Sci-Fi Visions

Animé films like *Nausicaä of the Valley of the Wind* (1984) and *Grave of the Fireflies* (1988) focus on survival after war and environmental disaster. In *Nausicaä of the Valley of the Wind*, the Princess Nausicaä must bring peace and restore the world's environment by facing up to the truth behind the catastrophic Seven Days of Fire and the mythical Sea of Corruption. Oshii's *Ghost in the Shell* (1995) and *Innocence: Ghost in the Shell 2* (2004), set in the future, look at the **cyborg** soul's dream of becoming human.

Final Fantasy: The Spirits Within (2001)

When aliens invade Earth, humans must find a way to destroy them. Using realistic computer-generated imagery (CGI), Final Fantasy urges for understanding instead of military might.

METROPOLIS (2001)

Inspired by Fritz Lang's masterpiece, Metropolis *depicts a city where robots live underground and humans live above ground. The film questions what it means to be human.*

FANTASY FOLKLORE

Fantasy animé films look back to the mysteries of Japanese folklore, rich in supernatural creatures, ghosts, and monsters. *Princess Mononoke* (1997) and *Spirited Away* (2001) focus on curses and grumpy gods in a fantasy world of spirits. *Princess Mononoke* has the animal gods of the forest battling against the iron miners who are exploiting their forest.

AKIRA (1998)

Based on the manga comics by Japanese director Katsuhiro Otomo, Akira follows Kaneda, the punk leader of a bike gang through Tokyo after World War III. While Kaneda's friend Tetsuo develops psychic powers, Kaneda discovers Akira, a top secret government project, which could lead to the end of the city. Exposing government corruption and the fear of nuclear holocaust, Akira started a trend for animé in the U.S. inspiring films like The Matrix *(1999).*

WALT DISNEY STUDIOS PRESENTS
A STUDIO GHIBLI FILM
MIYAZAKI'S
SPIRITED AWAY

SPIRITED AWAY (2002)

The first animé film to win an Academy Award®, Spirited Away *is the story of a girl, Chihiro, who struggles to free her greedy parents from a spell that turned them into pigs. A fantasy world filled with dragons, spirits, and gods reveals the greed of adults and the innocence of children.*

FILM TECHNOLOGY

STOP MOTION

Stop motion is a time consuming method used to animate models or three dimensional objects by creating a sequence frame by frame, filming one frame before altering the position of the model slightly and shooting the next. The illusion of live movement is created when the film is projected at normal speed.

TRAVELING MATTE

In order to create the spaceship battles in Star Wars (1977) a traveling matte is needed. First, a spaceship is filmed in front of a blue screen, invisible to color film. Two films called mattes are then created from this, one with a spaceship and the other with a spaceship-shaped hole. An optical printer is then used to combine the two mattes.

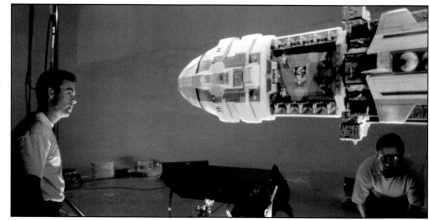

 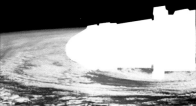 

COMPUTER GENERATED IMAGERY (CGI)

The realistic dinosaurs in Jurassic Park (1993) were created using CGI. The digital dinosaur begins as a wire skeleton. Layers of texture, such as skin, shadows, rain, and mud, are then added.

The digital model is then animated by clicking on the dinosaur's different joints. Once animated, the dinosaur can then be added to the live action sequences.

CGI wire model

CGI skins

Model ready for animating

GLOSSARY

atomic bomb
bomb whose explosive power comes from the smallest part of a chemical element that can possibly exist – an atom

clone
person or thing that looks like a replica of someone or something else

Cold War
state of tension between nations without an actual war. The term usually describes the situation between the Soviet Union and the U.S.A. between 1945 and 1991.

communism
political theory in which goods are shared equally

cyborg
something that has human biology but electronically-enhanced capabilities

evolution
term used to describe the development of species of animals and plants

film noir
film genre associated with violence and crime. Films are often set in the dark of night with rainy streets.

Great Depression
economic crisis that began with the stock market crash of 1929 and continued through the 1930s

humanoid
having an appearance or character like a human

nuclear holocaust
the end of the world as we know it as a result of a nuclear explosion

nuclear power
power, such as electricity produced by nucleur fusion. In sci-fi it is often shown to cause animal and human mutation.

patriotism
term that describes love of your country

satire
when humor is used to expose a weakness

Soviet Union
former collection of communist countries that was dissolved in 1991

totalitarian
state ruled by a government that demands complete obedience

INDEX